The Eloquent Peasant

The Eloquent Peasant

SECOND EDITION

Loren R. Fisher

CASCADE *Books* · Eugene, Oregon

THE ELOQUENT PEASANT
Second Edition

Cascade Books
A Division of Wipf and Stock Publishers
199 W. 8th Ave., Suite 3
Eugene, OR 97401

www.wipfandstock.com

ISBN 13: 978-1-62564-904-1

Cataloging-in-Publication data:

Fisher, Loren R.

    The eloquent peasant , second edition / Loren R. Fisher

    xvi + 64 p. ; 20.5 cm. Includes bibliographical references and index.

    ISBN 13: 978-1-62564-904-1

    1. Egyptian literature—Translations into English. 2. Eloquent Peasant. 3. Egypt—Civilization—To 332 B.C. I. Title.

PJ1531 E5 F5 2015

Manufactured in the USA

For Jane

The Egyptians said, "Thoth gave us writing."
Your gift is greater; you have made writing possible for me.

"Do for the doer to cause him to do." (B1 141)

"Do for the one who does for you." (B2 108)

"Overlook one blameworthy act, and it will become two." (B1 246)

"Speak Truth! Do Truth!" (B1 351)

Contents

Preface

The ancient Mediterranean world has given us many rich and colorful stories, and *The Eloquent Peasant* is by far one of my favorites. It is difficult for most of us to imagine a four-thousand-year-old story that considers the issues of social equality and the importance of perfect speech, but these issues are emphasized in this story. When the peasant went before the Chief Steward, his first speech amazed his audience. When this was reported to the Pharaoh, "His Majesty said, 'Since surely, you desire to see me, and that I am well (B1 110), you should cause him to delay here, without answering anything he says. In order to keep him speaking, be silent. Then it will be brought to us in writing that we may hear it.'" Egyptians were interested in rhetoric and the gift of writing.

The Gift of Writing

Who was D̲hwty? The Greeks called
   him Thoth.

Egyptians said that he gave them
   writing.

He invented it and some other things.

In Plato's *Phaedrus,* Thoth says as
   follows:

"Writing improves memory and
   wisdom."

But the King of Thebes said, "No" to
   all this.

"Rather, writing will destroy memory."

Is Plato jealous and thus critical?

The context in Plato is rhetoric.

Interesting. Egyptians loved great
   speech.

The Eloquent Peasant gave nine
   speeches.

Now, the King of Egypt said to Rensi,

"In order to keep him speaking, be
   silent.

Then it will be brought to us in writing

That we may hear it." And Rensi
   obeyed.

They were grateful for the gift of
   writing.

The Egyptians thought writing was
    helpful.
It was an aid to memory, praise Thoth.
It was a means of sharing and
    teaching.
It also provided entertainment.
When scribes took stories from oral
    telling,
The story was frozen, but it lived on.
The storyteller could compress or add
    to.
The written form does not rule; but it
    helps.

The structure of this story, right from the beginning, is built upon a series of speeches. This structure is well known in Hebrew literature. The book of Exodus is a prime example. See Exodus 4–14 and note the following: 4:1 "Moses answered; he said, . . . "; 4:6 "Yahweh said, . . . "; 4:10 "Moses said to Yahweh, . . . "; this goes on and on. The Egyptians taught most of the east Mediterranean world how to write, and it had to do with more than just structure. You will be able to see such things as commandments in *The Eloquent Peasant*, for example, "Do not steal" and "Do not covet."

Loren R. Fisher
10 May 2012
Medford, Oregon

Acknowledgments

The protesters in Tahrir Square brought to mind a four-thousand-year-old story from Egypt that related a peasant's search for equality. These events motivated me to accelerate my work on *The Eloquent Peasant*. I want to thank the protesters, and I wish them well.

For this work, I am indebted to the work of R. B. Parkinson.[1] In fact, it would have been impossible for me to translate this story without his book. He has moved the Egyptian text from the cursive Hieratic Egyptian to the formal Hieroglyphic Egyptian. He has also given us notes on the texts. In short, he has done the basic text-critical work for the translator. I thank him.

I am also dependant on the work of John Wilson and on his understanding of this story. In addition, the translations by F. O. Faulkner and Miriam Lichtheim have been helpful.

1. R. B. Parkinson, *The Tale of the Eloquent Peasant* (Oxford: Griffith Institute, Ashmolean Museum, 1991).

Acknowledgments

I want to thank my wife, Jane, for her careful editing and for her encouragement. K. C. Hanson, my editor at Cascade Books, has helped me in many ways to complete this project. Thanks K. C.

Abbreviations

ANET	*Ancient Near Eastern Texts,* edited by James B. Pritchard
ANEP	*The Ancient Near East In Pictures,* edited by James B. Pritchard
B1	Papyrus Berlin 3023
B2	Papyrus Berlin 3025
COS	*The Context of Scripture,* 3 vols., edited by William W. Hallo
Erman-Grapow	*Wörterbuch der ägyptischen Sprache*
Faulkner	"The Tale of the Eloquent Peasant"
Gardiner	*Egyptian Grammar,* 2nd ed.
Lichtheim	*Ancient Egyptian Literature,* vols. 1 and 2
Parkinson	*The Tale of Sinuhe and Other Egyptian Poems*

Abbreviations

R	Papyrus Ramesseum A, Papyrus Berlin 10499
Wilson	Translations in *ANET*

Introduction

On February 11, 2011, the Egyptian people experienced freedom and liberation as President Mubarak stepped down after thirty years of dictatorship over Egypt. The Egyptian people discovered that regime change is possible by nonviolence. True, three hundred people were killed and many more wounded by paid Mubarak thugs, but the protesters were willing to die for the freedom of the Egyptian people. This was a joyous event that did something for the people beyond the fulfillment of their demands; they gained a real sense of equality. There were laborers, doctors, lawyers, Muslims, Christians, and secularists. All rose up with one voice saying that Mubarak must go. The world hopes that these people are on the road to democracy, and most of them, for the first time, will experience a life that is defined by freedom from fear, freedom from the old regime, and freedom to fulfill their dreams.

Four thousand years ago a similar great moment occurred in Egypt's history. It happened toward the end of Egypt's First Intermediate Period before and during the Eleventh Dynasty (2135 to 2000 BCE). The downfall of the Old Kingdom, which was thought to be eternal, brought an end to material success and introduced anarchy and chaos. The Egyptian people had a difficult time with this change in their lives. The impact of these changes can be observed in *A Dialogue between a Man and His Ba*,[1] which was written in these chaotic times. In this story, the man argues with his *Ba* (or soul) about suicide.

Some positive works also came from this period. At Heracleopolis one of the kings wrote instructions to his son, Meri-ka-Re, emphasizing the need for reform. Meri-ka-Re's father taught him to do *ma'at*, "truth." Also the prophet Ipuwer said that the king should be a good shepherd rather than a wealthy lord. In his book on Egyptian culture, John Wilson writes, "The text which brings out most clearly the new approach to social equality and the new responsibility to render *ma'at* to one's fellows, rather than simply to the gods, is *The Story of the Eloquent Peasant*."[2]

1. For this story, see Fisher, *Tales from Ancient Egypt*.

2. Wilson, *The Culture of Ancient Egypt*, 120. Wilson's views have guided me in this discussion of The First

Wilson is correct. Equality and the hope for social justice is the fundamental theme in the story of *The Eloquent Peasant*, and this is why I have been interested in this story for some time.

The eloquent peasant, whose name is Khun-Anup, has much in common with the Egyptians in Tahrir Square. He was a poor peasant, who while taking his produce to market, was robbed, beaten, and belittled by Nemtinakht, who had the means and the connections to the bureaucracy to get away with such crimes. So the peasant appealed to the Chief Steward of the area. Now, it happens that this peasant's speech was truly beautiful, and after his first appeal the authorities did not answer. Instead, they enjoyed his speech and kept him around for more. He appealed nine times. He was tired of lies and falsehood; he demanded truth. At one point he says, "Do to the doer to make him do." This was an early form of the Golden Rule. He also says, "Doing justice is breath for the nose." Justice gives life, and it is a rare gift. He also predicts that a ruler may gain riches through falsehood, but his rule will be short lived. But with only silence from the authorities, the peasant became discouraged. He thought of suicide, and he was fearful.

Intermediate Period. See especially ibid., 120–24.

Finally, the authorities answered the peasant's appeals. The Chief Steward returned the peasant's goods and gave the property of Nemtinakht to him. At last the peasant was rewarded for standing for truth. As John Wilson says, "The point of the tale is that even the humblest of men may rise up and demand his rights."[3] Later, Wilson continues, "It would be pleasant if we could say that Egypt, having discovered the inherent value of the individual man, went on to try to give that concept greater validity and more effective force within the state. We cannot do so . . . When, under the national perils of the Second Intermediate Period and the aggressive nationalism of the Empire, the disciplined unity of the state became more important than the rights and opportunities of individuals, the concept of equality and social justice was finally swallowed up."[4]

To win freedom is a wonderful moment, but a people must be willing to guard that moment from those who would take it away in the name of loyalty and patriotism to the state and faithfulness to the altar.

3. Ibid., 122.
4. Ibid., 124.

Translation[1]

(R 1.1) <u>There was a man</u> whose name was Khun-Anup;[2] he was a peasant of the Field of Salt.[3] He had a wife whose name was [Me]ret.

<u>This peasant said to this wife of his</u>, "Now, [I] am going down to Egypt to [obtain] food there for my children. Go and measure the barley that is in the storehouse; bring the remainder of the barley as of [yesterday]." Then he measured for her [six] *heqat*[4] of barley.

(R 1.5) <u>This peasant said to this wife of his</u>, "Now, [there are] twenty *heqat* of barley for food, for you and for your children, but you shall

---

1. This translation begins with text R, and I underline those phrases that are underlined in the text. The line numbers follows Parkinson's numbering system. Text B1 becomes my basic text starting with B1 33.

2. Khun-Anup means, "Anubis protects."

3. Wadi Natron.

4. A *heqat* is just a little more than a gallon.

make for me these six *heqa*t of barley into bread and beer[5] for every day [so I can live] on it."

This peasant went down to Egypt (B1 1) after he loaded his donkeys with: reeds,[6] *redemet* plants, natron, salt, (B1 5) sticks from [Hes]tiu,[7] wood from Farafra, panther hides, jackal hides, *nesha* plants, (B1 10) *'anw* stones, *tenem* plants, *khprwr* plants, *s3hwt* plants, *miswt* plants, *snt* stones, *'bw* stones, *ibs3* plants, *inbi* plants, pigeons, *n'rw* birds, *wgsw* birds, *wbn* plants, *tbsw* plants, *gngnt*, *shni-t3*, and *inst*—(B1 15) a full (load) of all the good products of the Field of Salt.

This peasant went south[8] toward Ninsu.[9] He arrived in the region of Per-Fefi to the north of Medenit. He found a man standing upon the riverbank, whose name was Nemtinakht.[10] (B1 20) He was the son of a man whose name was

5. Homan, "Beer and Its Drinkers."

6. All these items are in a vertical column of twenty-seven lines in the Egyptian text.

7. Faulkner, 32.

8. Literally, "sailed upstream."

9. This is Heracleopolis, and it was the capital of Egypt in 2155–2050 BCE (Ninth and Tenth Dynasties).

10. Nemtinakht means, "Nemti is strong." This name was read by Wilson and Gardiner as Thut-Nakht or Thoth-Nakht. They read Gardiner's sign list G26, the sacred ibis, instead of Nemti.

Isry, and he was one of the serfs of the Chief Steward,[11] Rensi, the son of Meru.

This Nemtinakht said, when he saw the donkeys of this peasant, which were desirable in his heart, indeed, he said,[12] "I wish I had a powerful[13] divine image; I would steal this peasant's goods with it."

(B1 25) Now the house of this Nemtinakht was on the shoreline by a path—it was narrow; it was not wide—it measured the width of a loincloth. His[14] path's one side was under water, the other under barley.

This Nemtinakht said to his follower, "Go bring me a shroud[15] from my house." It was

11. The Chief Steward (literally, "overseer of the estate") was a high official. See Ward, "The Egyptian Office of Joseph," for a discussion of official titles in the Egyptian government.

12. "He said" is in B1 but not in R.

13. "Powerful" is in B1 but not in R.

14. "His" refers to Nemtinakht. Most translations just translate, "Its one side was under water, . . ." "His path" is in the text, however, and it does add a bit of color. Nemtinakht claims it as his own.

15. "Shroud" or *Lanken* is what is given in Erman-Grapow, 1:71. Most translations give "cloth" or "sheet," but in this story death is very present. Also, it is worth mentioning that Egyptian *sm3-t3* ("shoreline") is the place where the earth is buried by the water. In fact, the Egyptian also refers to a person reaching the land or being

brought to him at once. (B1 30) Then he spread it out on the shoreline path; its hem settled on the water and its woven edge on the barley. This peasant came on the public path.[16]

This Nemtinakht said, "Peasant! Take it easy. Do not step[17] on my garments."

This peasant said, "I shall do your pleasure; my way is good." (B1 35) He went up higher.

This Nemtinakht said, "Is my Upper Egyptian[18] barley a path[19] for you?"

This peasant said, "Good are my ways. The riverbank is high, and the only ways are under the Upper Egyptian barley. You certainly ordered the closure of our path with your garments. Will you not allow our passage on the path?"[20]

---

buried. This may be suggesting a bit much, but in a few lines (B1 58), the peasant's life is threatened by Nemtinakht. Could our author be thinking of a shroud-covered path leading to burial and death?

16. "Public path" is from "a path for all the people." In n. 14, I suggest that it is claimed by Nemtinakht as his own, but it is not his.

17. From this point I follow text B1, but I will still do the underlining as in text R and look to R for help.

18. "Upper Egyptian" is not in R.

19. R has "path of a peasant."

20. R has an extra phrase at this point, and it reads: "As he finished speaking, . . ."

(B1 40) Then one of these donkeys filled its mouth with a wisp of the Upper Egyptian barley.

<u>This Nemtinakht said</u>, "Look, I will take away your donkey, peasant, because it is eating my Upper Egyptian barley. Note, it will tread (out the grain) because of its harvesting."[21]

<u>This peasant said</u>, "My ways are good. (B1 45) Only one (wisp) is destroyed, and for its price,[22] I will buy back[23] my donkey if you take it for filling its mouth with a wisp of Upper Egyptian barley. Now I know the Lord of this district; it belongs to the Chief Steward, Rensi, son of Meru. Now he is the one who punishes every thief in this entire land. Shall I be robbed in his district?"

(B1 50) <u>This Nemtinakht said</u>, "Is this the proverb that people are saying: 'A poor man's

21. The donkey harvested by eating. Most translations are: "because of its offence," but this only works if the determinative is G37 (a sparrow). The use of Z9 changes the meaning to an act of harvesting.

22. For this translation, I have followed the work of Wente, "A Note on *The Eloquent Peasant*, B I, 13–15."

23. "Buy" is not the basic meaning of the verb. It usually means, "to bring." Wilson's incomplete translation is still of value: "(Only) one (wisp) has been damaged. I brought my donkey because of . . . ; wilt thou take him for filling his mouth with a wisp of grain?" See Wilson, "The Protests of the Eloquent Peasant," 408.

name is pronounced on account of his Lord?' I am speaking to you, and you call forth the Chief Steward."[24]

Then he took a stick of green tamarisk to him, and he beat all his limbs with it, took away his donkeys, (B1 55) and brought (them) to his estate. Then this peasant wept very loudly because of the pain of that which was done to him.

This Nemtinakht said, "Do not raise your voice, peasant. Look, you belong to the abode of the Lord of Silence."[25]

This peasant said, "You beat me; you steal my goods; you even take away the (B1 60) complaint from my mouth. O Lord of Silence, give me my property. Then I will not wail (because of) the fear of you."

This peasant spent a week,[26] that is, ten days, appealing to this Nemtinakht, but he did not

24. Nemtinakht is using a bit of false humility as he identifies himself with the poor. According to him, the peasant should have called him by name. Instead, the peasant bypasses Nemtinakht and invokes his Lord. This angers Nemtinakht. A person's name is very important as can be seen in the first poem in *A Dialogue between a Man and His Ba* where the man says, "Look, my name stinks!" See Fisher, *Tales from Ancient Egypt*, 79 and n. 32.

25. The Lord of Silence is Osiris, God of the dead. Nemtinakht is threatening murder.

26. This word in Egyptian means "period," but it is

give his approval to it. So this peasant went[27] to Ninsu to appeal[28] to the Chief Steward, (B1 65) Rensi, son of Meru. He found him coming out of the door of his house to go down to his boat from the court.[29]

This peasant said, "Would that I be given permission to inform you about this dispute, and may a minister of your choice be allowed to come to me whom I might send back (B1 70) to you concerning it."

So the Chief Steward, Rensi, son of Meru, allowed his minister of his choice to go before him, and this peasant sent him back with every detail about this dispute. Then the Chief Steward, Rensi, son of Meru, accused this Nemtinakht to the officials who were with him.

(B1 75) They said to him,[30] "Surely, this is a peasant of his, who ran away to another beside him. Look, that is what they do to their peas-

---

followed by the number ten, which acts as a determinative. Therefore, I translate it "week." The Egyptian week had ten days. Others think that this "ten" is an error.

27. R inserts "south" here.

28. R inserts "it."

29. The Egyptian word here refers to the gate where court cases are judged. The court provides this high official with this boat.

30. This is Rensi.

ants, who have gone to others beside them. Yes, that is what they do! Is there cause to punish this Nemtinakht on account of a little natron with a little salt? (B1 80) If he is commanded to replace it, he will replace it."

The Chief Steward, Rensi, son of Meru, was silent. He did not answer these officials, nor did he answer this peasant.

The First Appeal

Then this peasant came to appeal to the Chief Steward, Rensi, son of Meru.[31] He said:

"O Chief Steward, my Lord, greatest of the great, (B1 85) guide to all that does not exist and to all that does exist.[32]

---

31. Text R inserts at this point *sp tpy*, "the first time." *Tpy* is an adjective form of *tp*, "head." This usage is not surprising, but it is interesting; and Hebrew with its adjective form (*rishon*) from "head" is used in the same way. There will be nine speeches that are numbered, so the insertion from R makes sense.

32. Antonymous pairs are used many times to mean "everything." You can also see this in pairs like "good and evil." See Fisher, *Genesis, A Royal Epic*, and the note to Genesis 2:17. It reads: "The "knowledge of good and evil" means the "knowledge of everything." See Genesis 3:5, 22; 31:24. The passage that makes it all clear is 2 Samuel 14:17 and 20 (in v. 17 David can understand "good and evil" and hence in v. 20 he knows everything).

When you go down to the Lake of *Ma'at*,[33]

You will sail on it with a good wind.

No part of your sail will be torn,

Nor will your ship stall.

No disaster will befall your mast

Nor break your yards.

You will not be too powerful,

Nor will you run aground. (B1 90)

You will not be carried away by a wave;

You will not taste the evil of the river.

You will not behold fear.[34]

Darting fish will come to you.

You will catch fat birds.

For you are a father to the orphan,

A husband to the widow,

A brother to the divorced,

And (B1 95) a cloak to the one who is not a
    mother.[35]

33. "*Ma'at*" means "truth/justice," and it is important
to the peasant and his arguments.

34. Several translations have some variations of "You
shall not see the face of fear." However, what they translate as "face" is usually a preposition, "on" or "at," and I
understand it that way. However, text R gives support for
reading "face" because it has added the preposition *n* after
the glyph for face. Text R seems to add things that expand
the text. See n. 31 above. But usually the more difficult
reading is to be preferred.

35. In Ancient Mediterranean Literature it is said

Let me make your name in this land according to every good law:

> A leader free from malicious greed,
>
> A great one free from wickedness,
>
> One who destroys falsehood,
>
> One who creates truth,
>
> And one who comes to the cry of him who gives voice.[36]

I speak that you may hear; (B1 100) create truth, O praised one, whom the praised ones praise. Take away my[37] needs. Look at me! I am burdened down.[38] Examine me! See, I am at loss.[39]"

Now this peasant made this speech in the time of the Majesty of the King of Upper and

---

again and again that the good king cares for the widow and the orphan.

36. Here I follow the lead of John Wilson and his translation. It also reminds me of the rebel Job who asks, "Who hears the cries of the innocent?" These five statements refer to great names like the five names given in a royal titulary to the kings of Egypt. The fifth one is replaced by text R; it is replaced with "Throw evil to the earth."

37. The "my" is from text R.

38. R adds, "with sorrow. Look at me! I am weak over it."

39. R has "in trouble" instead of "at loss."

Lower Egypt, Nebkaure, the justified.[40] The Chief Steward, Rensi, son of Meru, (B1 105) went before his Majesty.

He said, "My lord, I have found one from these peasants whose beautiful speech is a reality.[41] His goods were stolen,[42] and he has come to appeal to me about it.

His Majesty said, "Since surely, you desire to see me, and that I am well,[43] (B1 110) you should

40. In Gardiner, *Egypt of the Pharaohs*, 112, there is a helpful discussion of the Heracleopolitan dynasties nine and ten (2155–2050 BCE) and the House of Akhtoy, in which we know of at least three kings. The third king is known from a weight excavated by Petrie. He is Akhtoy Nebkaure, and Gardiner relates him to *The Story of the Eloquent Peasant.* For the meaning of "the justified," see Montet, *Everyday Life in Egypt*, 306, where Montet deals with *maa kherou*, "just of voice." There may be a few exceptions, but it is after one's death that he is declared "just of voice" or "justified." So this story is placed in the time of King Nebkaure by the storyteller. Wilson, in *The Culture of Ancient Egypt*, 114, places our story before 2000 BCE.

41. Perfect speech is admired in Egyptian didactic literature. Note Wilson's translation of *The Instructions of Ptah-hotep* in *ANET*, 412, "Good speech is more hidden than the emerald, but it may be found with maidservants at the grindstones." Also see ibid., 415, "be a craftsman in speech," from *The Instruction for King Meri-Ka-Re*.

42. At this point text R adds: "by a man who is my opponent."

43. This underlining is in B1; R only underlines "His

cause him to delay here, without answering anything he says. In order to keep him speaking, be silent. Then it will be brought to us in writing that we may hear it.[44] But provide that on which his wife and children may live.[45] Note, one of these peasants (comes) just before his house is empty to the ground.[46] In addition, keep alive this peasant himself. You shall cause food to be given to him (B1 115) without letting him know that you are the one who has given it to him.[47] Then ten loaves of bread and two jugs of beer were given to him every day. It was Rensi, the Chief Steward, son of Meru, who gave them. He gave them to his friend, and it was he who gave them to him. Then Rensi, the Chief Steward, son of Meru sent [a message][48] to the mayor of Field

---

Majesty said."

44. R's version is short: "so that his speech will be brought to us in writing." Note that it is important to write things down. Oral reporting is not enough.

45. For the translation of this sentence, I follow Wilson, *ANET*, 409. Text R has: "But provide that on which the wife of this peasant may live."

46. His cupboards are bare. He is down to rock bottom.

47. R adds a note here that will be covered in B1, 116 and 117.

48. The text does not have "a message" or "a messenger," but we need it in translation unless we follow Lichtheim and change "send" to "wrote." This is not a difficult

of Salt about providing food for the wife of this peasant consisting of three *heqat* of barley every day.[49]

The Second Appeal

<u>Then this peasant came to appeal to him a second time</u>. He said:

"O Chief Steward, my Lord, greatest of the great, (B1 120) richest of the rich, who is greater than his great ones, richer than his rich ones!

> Oar of Heaven,
>
> Beam of Earth,
>
> And plumb-line that carries a weight.
>
> Oar, do not go astray.
>
> Beam, do not tilt.
>
> Plumb-line, do not move off center.

A great lord takes possession only of that which does not have an owner, plundering that

---

problem. In Hebrew prose we encounter the same thing. In Genesis 31:4 note, "Jacob sent [a messenger/a message]," but in 32:4, "Jacob sent messengers ahead of him." The object can be left out or included. Also see Genesis 27:42.

49. Here R inserts another repetitious note.

alone.[50] Your rations are in your house:[51] (B1 125) a jar of beer with three loaves of bread. What more do you need to spend to satisfy your dependants? Indeed a mortal man dies[52] with his household; <u>will you be an immortal?</u>[53] Indeed, is it not wrong, a balance that tilts, a plummet that strays, and the truly loyal one who becomes disconnected?

> Look! Justice flees [from those] under you; [it is] expelled from its place:
>
> Officials are doing evil;
>
> Crafty speech shows partiality; (B1 130)
>
> Judges rob what has been seized;
>
> He who twists speech from its accurate sense makes himself crooked from it;
>
> He who gives breath is short of breath on earth;
>
> He who rests makes himself breath;

50. This is close to the translation in Faulkner, 36. The next 25 lines are only from text B1.

51. See Gardiner, 93, 7.

52. "A mortal man dies" from Egyptian $m(w)t\ m(w)t$. This is stylistic and poetic. $M(w)t$ is Egypto-Semitic. This root is used in Hebrew, Ugaritic, Akkadian, and other Semitic languages. The basic meaning is "death." But it can also be used for "man," "woman," "Mot" (at Ugarit the god of death), Egyptian Mut is a goddess at Thebes, wife of Amun, and $m(w)t$ also means, "mother."

53. Literally, "a man of eternity."

The arbitrator is one who defrauds;

The one who expels need commands its
   creation;

The town is flooded;

And he who punishes crime does evil."

The Chief Steward, Rensi, son of Meru, said,
(B1 135) "Is that which is on your mind more important to you than your being seized by my follower?"

This peasant said:

"The measurer of the grain-heaps cheats for
   himself;

He who fills for another cheats that neighbor;

And he who rules by the laws[54] commands
   theft.

Who then shall redress misery?

He who removes weakness acts corruptly;

He who corrects another is crooked;

And he who talks about another is a doer of
   evil.

What do you find for yourself? (B1 140)

Short is redress; long is evil.

A good reputation returns to its place of
   yesterday.[55]

This is the precept:

54. The Egyptians did have laws even if we do not have a code.

55. Or perhaps "is remembered."

'*Do for the doer to cause him to do.*'[56]

This is thanking God for him and for what he
     may do;

This is deflecting an arrow[57] before it is shot;

This is commissioning an item[58] to a master
     artist.[59]

Would that a moment would bring its
     destruction:[60]

Spilling your foul wine,[61]

Decreasing your fowls,

And mutilating your marsh-birds.

The one who watches has become blind.

56. Here we have it: "Do unto others . . ." Also in the
ninth appeal we have a related saying: "Do for him who
does for you" (B2 108).

57. I translate "arrow," but the word is "thing."

58. Again the literal meaning is "thing."

59. "Master artist" from "master workman."

60. Here the positive approach is reversed to the realm
of reality. Why? The peasant is disgusted because the
"Golden Rule" has not been the basis of action. Instead
there has been ill-gotten gain, which should be destroyed.
The following lines explain the details of this wish for
destruction.

61. This is a difficult line. The boat determinative
should be turned over for "upset" or "spill," and others
translate "vineyard" and "bird-nets" instead of "diseased
or foul wine." The above translation is a step in the right
direction.

The one who listens is deaf, (B1 145)

And the leader has become one who leads astray.

. . . [62] <u>Pray, are you healthy?</u>

<u>Why do you act against yourself?</u>

Look, You are strong; your arm is powerful; your heart is greedy,

And kindness is beyond you.

How grievous is the miserable one whom you have destroyed. (B1 150)

You are like the messenger of the Crocodile God.[63]

Look,[64] you have surpassed the Lady of Pestilence![65]

If you have nothing, she has nothing.

If she has nothing,[66] there is nothing for you.

62. I have not solved the problem with the unknown Egyptian word *ʿnbrw*.

63. This is Khenty, a crocodile god of death.

64. Text R begins again at this point.

65. This is the lion goddess, Sekhmet. For me the following poem seems to devalue the role of Sekhmet and the blame is put on Rensi. I have reproduced this poem in Egyptian to show not only the poetic structure but also the visual impact.

66. Some insert the Egyptian preposition *r* in this first phrase to make it the same as the second phrase, i.e., "If there is nothing *for* her."

If you do not do it, it is not done.[67]"

"The lord of bread should be kind; might belongs to the criminal. Stealing is common among those who do not have possessions. (B1 155) Stealing possessions by the criminal is an evil deed of one without need. Should not he be blamed? He is seeking for himself. Thus, you are sated with your bread; you are drunk with your beer; you are rich with all things.[68]

"The helmsman faces forward, but the boat drifts as it pleases. The king is confined; the rudder is in your power,[69] but evil exists in your environment. (B1 160) My appeal is long; my departure is difficult. 'What is with him who is there?' they will say."

67. In this last phrase some insert a pronominal suffix as the subject and translate, "*she* does not do it." This is possible, but I prefer to translate the text as I have it.

68. This paragraph is not easy to translate. I hope that I have given a better translation and understanding than some others, and I avoided the need for some common emendations.

69. "Power" is literally "arm" but not "hand" as several translate. If the word were "hand" I would still go with "power."

nn n.k nn n.s

If you have nothing, she has nothing.

nn s nn r.k

If she has nothing, there is nothing for you.

n ìrr.k st n ìrr st

If you do not do it, it is not done.

From B1 150–155 in the peasant's second appeal, Rensi is the one to be feared and more so than the Lady of Pestilence, i.e., Sekhmet. In the third line of this poem, it is clearly Rensi who causes the misery of the poor. The two negative hieroglyphs in each line cast their negative spell on Rensi. The negative sign consists of both arms outspread with palms up proclaiming without a word, "nothing." A new title: "Don't Blame The Gods. Blame Rensi."

"Make a refuge, and your harbor will be
    healthy.

Look, your town is surrounded by crocodiles.

Precise be your tongue; you shall not go astray.

This serpent[70] in man is his limb.[71]

<u>Do not tell lies! Beware of officials!</u>

This basket fattens the judges.[72] (B1 165)

Telling lies is their herbs;

It lies lightly on their hearts.

Wisest of all mankind, do you not know of my
    situation?

You who meets the need of all upon the water,

Look, I am underway without a ship.

You who brings to the harbor all who are
    drowning,[73] (B1 170)

Save the shipwrecked; save[74] me within the
    limits of your area."

70. Here I follow Lichtheim. This Egyptian word *t3mw*
is difficult, but it has the serpent determinative.

71. "Limb" probably refers to his "tongue,"

72. "Basket" might refer to a "basket full of bribes."
The rest of this appeal presents us with a situation where
much of the translation contains a lot of guesswork.

73. After this text R 26.4–6 adds: "Behold, I am loaded
with sorrow. Behold, I am in your power; take account of
me. Behold, I am in pain."

74. At this point, Text B1 169 has *ḥdr*, which seems to
be unknown, and so I have gone with text R 26.7 where
this unknown word is replaced with *šd*, which is also used

The Third Appeal

<u>Then this peasant came to appeal to him a third time</u>; he said:

"Chief Steward, my lord, you are Re, Lord of the sky, along with your entourage. Everyone's sustenance is from you just like the flood. You are Hâpi,[75] who makes green the meadows and re-establishes the destroyed fields.

> (B1 175) Punish robbery, save the wretched,
> And do not become a flood[76] against those who appeal.
> Desire to endure, as it is said:
> 'Doing justice![77] This is breath in the nose.'[78]
> Complete the punishment against him who is punished;
> No one will surpass your correctness.
> Will the hand-balance err? (B1 180)

---

as the first word in this line. It means to "save" or "rescue."

75. This god is the God of the Nile and creates by means of the inundation the possibility of agriculture.

76. Rensi is praised as a good flood that provides food, but he is not to be a destructive flood against one who was robbed.

77. Or "truth."

78. The context is different, but the importance of "breath" is similar to Genesis 2:7 where Yahweh-Elohim blows into the human's nostrils and "The human becomes a living being."

Will the stand-balance tilt to the side?

Will Thoth be lenient?[79] Then you could do evil.

<u>You shall make yourself equal</u> to these three.[80]

If these three are lenient, then you can be lenient.

Do not answer good with bad.

Do not put one thing in the place of another.

Speech grows more than stinkweeds (B1 185) in order to attack the smeller with answers. The one who waters evil makes the cover-up grow. This is three times now to make him act.[81]

Place your steering oar according to the sail.[82]

Draw back the flood in order to do justice.[83]

Beware lest you move upon the tiller rope. (B1 190)

Making equal the land is doing justice.[84]

79. The expected answer is, "No."

80. That is, Thoth, the balance, and the stand-balance.

81. The peasant has appealed three times to Rensi.

82. In this allegory the ruler is a good sailor and also in the following lines a balance or scale that weighs ones actions against truth/justice. This line is followed by an interpretive line. The poetic nature of these lines is clear. "The sail," "the tiller rope," and "making equal" all have the same endings: *ndbyt*, *nfryt*, and *ꜥk3yt*.

83. Or "truth."

84. Or "truth."

Do not speak a falsehood for you are great.

Do not be a lightweight for you are weighty.

Do not speak a falsehood for you are a
balance.

Do not act confused for you are the chief.

Look, you are the main one like the balance.

If it tilts, you may tilt.

Do not stray; take the oar; (B1 195) pull on the
tiller rope.

Do not rob;[85] take action against the robber.

Not great is the great one who is covetous.

Your tongue is the plummet;

Your heart is the weight;

Your lips are its arms.[86]

If you turn your face from the mighty, who
will oppose misery?[87] (B1 200)

Look, you are a miserable washerman,

A covetous one, who destroys a friend,

One who wrongs his intimate[88] for his inferior
client.

85. These commandments remind one of the Ten Commandments in Exodus 20:1–14: "Thou shall not steal" with "covetous" in the near context.

86. Since the ruler is like a balance, his tongue, heart and lips make up the various parts.

87. This presupposes that the "mighty" are the ones who create "misery." The word for "misery" is also used in the next line.

88. For "intimate" or trusted friend see Fisher, *Tales*

This is his brother; one who comes with gifts
for him.

Look, you are a ferryman, who ferries all who
pay,

A right acting one whose rightness has been
torn asunder. (B1 205)

Look, you are the chief of the storehouse,

Who will not allow passage to one who is
empty handed.

Look, you are a hawk to the common people,

One who lives on helpless birds.

Look you are a butler, whose joy is butchering,

Since the mutilation is not an act against him.

Look, you are a herdsman. Is it not bad for me
that you cannot count?[89] (B1 210)

[If you could count] you would become less
than a greedy crocodile.

Refuge shelter(s) have been destroyed for the
town(s) in the entire land.

Hearer! You do not really hear. Why do you
not hear?

---

from Ancient Egypt, 81 n. 34, where an "intimate" is literally "one who enters the heart." Here a different word is used, but the use of "intimate" and "brother" was important is this literature.

89. A shepherd needs to be able to count his flock when he brings his sheep into the shelter. Parkinson, 81 n. 53, comes close to this understanding.

Today, I really opposed the aggressor, and the crocodile retreated. Now, what help is this to you? The hiding place of truth will be found, and falsehood will run away to the ground.[90] Do not prepare for tomorrow before it comes; (B1 215) one does know the evil in it.[91]

Now this peasant gave this speech to the Chief Steward, Rensi, the son of Meru, at the gate of the hall of judgment. Then [Rensi][92] sent two guards to him with whips, and they beat all his limbs with them.

This peasant said, "The son of Meru goes on erring. His face[93] is blind to what he sees and deaf to what he hears. (B1 220) [His] mind[94] wanders from what is recalled to him.

Look, you are like a village with no headman,

90. *Rdi s3* means, "to turn the back or flee." Falsehood does not have a "back" as is assumed in many translations, but falsehood does flee from the truth.

91. In this line the words "comes" and "evil" are both spelled *iit* but with different determinatives (legs walking and the sparrow). This sort of thing is done in poetry and high prose. There are other ways dealing with evil or trouble.

92. The text has "he."

93. "Face" could also be translated as "being" or "person."

94. "Mind" is better in this context than "heart." In Egyptian *ib* can mean "heart" or "mind."

Like a crowd with no leader,
Like a boat with no captain,
Confederates with no leader.

Look, you are a "judge"[95] who steals,
A headman who is bribed,
An overseer who punishes plundering,
Who has become an icon for the evildoer."[96]

The Fourth Appeal

(B1 225) Then this peasant came to appeal to him a fourth time. He found him coming out from the gate of the temple of Arsaphés.[97] He said, "O praised one, may Arsaphés praise you, from whose temple you have come.

Goodness is demolished!
Its unity does not exist,
To throw back falsehood to the ground.[98]

95. This may be a best guess. The basic meaning of the Egyptian word is "dispute."

96. "Evildoer" is literally, "doer against man."

97. Also rendered as Herishef, Harsaphes, and Arsaphes. This is the ram god of Heracleopolis.

98. For "throw back falsehood to the ground" see n. 90 above. Here *s3*, "back" is also used, and it does not refer to "falsehood's back," but it becomes part of the verbal element.

(B1 230) Has the ferry gone under? How does one make a crossing when it becomes a dreadful crossing? Is crossing the river on sandals a good crossing?[99] No! Nothing at all. Who now can sleep until dawn? Perished is walking by night, traveling by day, and helping a man stand up for his own good actions to establish truth. (B1 235)

> Look, it is no use to tell you this.
> Kindness has passed you by.
> How grievous is the wretched one whom you
>   have destroyed.
> Look, you are a hunter,[100] who calms his
>   heart,[101]
> Who gives way to do as he pleases:
> Spearing hippopotamuses, shooting bulls,
> Catching fish, and snaring birds.

> (B1 240) There is no one, who is quick to
>   speak that is free from rashness.

99. These three questions are difficult to translate. The second question is my best guess.

100. The Egyptian means, "one who spears fish," but in light of what follows he is more than a "fisherman."

101. "Calm his heart" is literally, "wash his heart." For a discussion of the meaning of this phrase see Lichtheim, "The Instruction of Ptahhotep," 1:77 n. 9. She says that to wash the heart is "to relieve the heart of feelings."

There is no one, who is light-hearted that is
    slow to move on bodily desires.[102]

Be patient so that you may know the truth.

Subdue your choice for the good of the one
    who enters humbly.

There is no one, who is impetuous[103] who at-
    tains excellence.

There is no one, who is quick of mind who will
    exist.

Come, let the eyes see, and may the heart be
informed. (B1 245) Do not be harsh correspond-
ing to your power lest evil come to thee. Overlook one blameworthy act, and it will become
two. It is the eater who tastes, and the one who
is questioned who answers. It is the sleeper who
sees the dream. 'As for the judge who ought to be
punished, he is a pattern for the (wrong)-doer.'[104]

(B1 250) Fool, look! You are attacked.

Ignorant one, look! You are questioned.

You who bails water, look! You have entered.[105]

102. See Gardiner, 83 n. 9, for discussion of this.

103. Here I follow Faulkner, 42. This section of six lines
is very difficult, and the translations are very different.

104. This quotation is from Gardiner, 312 n. 11. Also
see above, line [224], where I translated "role-model" for
"pattern." Also Gardiner uses "criminal" for "(wrong)-
doer" in Gardiner, 93 n. 13.

105. Perhaps this means, "You are permitted to enter

Helmsman, do not let go astray your boat.

Giver of life, do not let die.

Provider,[106] do not let perish.

Shade, do not let in the sun. (B1 255)

Shelter, do not let the crocodile seize.

The fourth appeal to you, shall I spend all day at it?"

The Fifth Appeal

And this peasant came to appeal to him a fifth time. He said, "Chief Steward, my Lord! The *hwdw*-fisherman [. . .] the *mhyt*-[fish].[107] The [*n*]*yw*-fisherman is killing the *iy*-fish. (B1 260) The fish-spearer is spearing the *iwbbw*-fish. The *d3bhrw*-fisherman is after the *p3krw*-fish. The *whc*-fisherman is destroying the river.

Look, you are like such a one! Do not defraud the poor of his belongings, a powerless one whom you know.[108] His belongings are breath to the wretched (B1 265) and to take them away

---

the boat."

106. For this meaning see Erman-Grapow, 3:196; and Lichtheim, 183 n. 22.

107. The text is damaged here, but perhaps it could be restored following the pattern of the next few lines.

108. Here the peasant seems to be referring to himself.

stops up the nose.[109] You were appointed to hear litigations, to judge between two, and to punish the robber.

Look! Supporting the thief is that which you have done. Trust has been placed in you, and you have become a transgressor. You were appointed to be a dam for the poor and to protect him from drowning.

(B1 270) Look! You are his lake that drags him under."

The Sixth Appeal

And this peasant came to appeal to him a sixth time. He said, "Chief Steward, my Lord! A Lord[110]

109. Here I do not follow Parkinson, 69. He translates, "taking them [i.e., his belongings] is suffocating him." This is not the case at all. The ancients tested the flow of breath from the nose to see if someone was alive. Taking one's belongings was such a horrible act it was tantamount to killing the poor man; there would be no breath coming out his nose. So taking his belongings is not "suffocating" the poor man, but rather it is *killing* him—perhaps from a stroke or whatever. When tested, he would be pronounced dead.

110. Or perhaps delete "Lord" and translate "He."

who corrects[111] falsehood is the creator of Truth; he creates all goodness and destroys all <evil>.[112]

> Like when satiety comes and ends hunger[113]
> (as) clothing ends nakedness.[114] (B1 275)
> Like when the sky is at rest after a strong storm
>   and warms everyone who is cold.
> Like when fire cooks the raw.
> Like when water quenches thirst.
> See for yourself!
> He who divides is one who defrauds. (B1 280)
> He who should bring contentment is causing
>   trouble.
> He who restores is causing suffering.
> He who cheats diminishes Truth;
> Fill exactly; Truth is not deficient or
>   overflowing.[115]

If you acquire, give to your brothers, (B1 285) for such eating[116] would lack[117] equality. My trouble leads to separation; my accuser brings about departure. One cannot know what exists

111. See Erman-Grapow, 4:40.

112. Most translators insert "all evil."

113. See Gardiner, 379 n. 9.

114. See Erman-Grapow, 3:14.

115. Text B2 adds, "So do likewise."

116. Literally, "chewing."

117. Literally, "emptiness."

in the heart. Do not delay! You should act on the report. If you are torn away, who will remain?[118] The staff to test the waters is in your hand[119] like a pole that helps[120] when a bad occasion happens at sea. (B1 290) If a boat runs aground it can be salvaged, but its cargo perishes on the ground all along the riverbank.

> You are educated,
> You are enlightened,
> And you are complete.
> Indeed, but not in order to defraud,
> You act like everyone;
> Your neighborhood is crooked, equally by everyone.
> Cheater of the entire land,
> Gardener of wickedness,
> He is watering his garden with evil. (B1 295)
> He makes his garden grow with falsehood
> And waters trouble unto eternity."

The Seventh Appeal

And this peasant came to appeal to him a seventh time. He said, "Chief Steward, my Lord:

118. Or who will be "tied" or "bound."

119. My translation "tests" is from a verb, which means to "fight."

120. This is a pole that is "open" or "free" to be used.

You are the steering-oar of the entire land.
The land sails in accordance with your
    command.
You are a second Thoth;[121] (B1 300)
The judge, who is not partial.

My Lord, may you permit a man to call on you concerning the rightness of his action. Do not be angry; it is not for you. The farsighted one has become shortsighted.[122] Do not brood over what has not yet come; do not rejoice over what has not yet happened. Patience protects friendship; it destroys a past event, which happened, and one cannot know what was in the heart. (B1 305) O one who breaks the law! O one who destroys right order! No poor man can live, when he is robbed. Truth does not address him.

Now my body was full; my heart was burdened. It all came from my body because of this

121. Thoth was the god of hieroglyphic writing and the god of wisdom and learning. He also participated as judge in the weighing of the heart on judgment day.

122. This line has two Egyptian expressions: "long of heart/mind" and "short of heart/mind." The first one is followed by the word "sight" and hence the translation, "farsighted," and its opposite would be "shortsighted." Since the word for heart can also mean, "mind" the line could also mean, "The thoughtful one has become thoughtless."

condition.[123] As with a breach in a dam, whose water flows out, so my mouth opened to speak. (B1 310) Then I used my pole of red cedar;[124] I bailed out my water;[125] I expelled that which was in my body; and I washed my linen. My speech has been completed. My misery ended up before you. Now what do you need? Your idleness leads you astray. Your greed will make you foolish; your gluttony will create your enemies. But, will you find another peasant like me? (B1 315) Is there an idle one where one who appeals will stand before the door of his house?

> There is none who is silent for whom you have enabled his speech.
>
> There is none who is sleeping whom you have caused to wake up.
>
> There is none who is overwhelmed whom you have prepared.
>
> There is none who is "shut-of-mouth" whom you have opened.[126]

123. "This condition" refers to the robbery and his confinement.

124. The "red cedar pole," perhaps from Syria, takes us back to boating terminology for weathering a storm as we encountered in B1 288.

125. Here "my water" refers to urine.

126. See Lichtheim, 2:120, for "The Opening of the Mouth" ritual. It is Ptah who opens the mouth of the dead. The dead also need nourishment.

There is none who is ignorant whom you have
increased his knowledge.

There is none who is foolish whom you have
taught.

Officials are dispellers of evil, lords of goodness, (B1 320) craftsmen who create what is, and
ones who tie up severed heads."[127]

The Eighth Appeal

And this peasant came to appeal to him an
eighth time. He said, "Chief Steward, my Lord!
One falls low through greed. A greedy man is
free from success. His success exists in failure.
You are greedy! Your heart is covetous! You steal,
and it is not beneficial for you. So, help a man

---

127. To "tie up severed heads" probably means, "to
bundle up these trophies of victory in battle." Gordon in
The World of the Old Testament, 154, writes, "In Ugarit,
Mesopotamia, and Egypt cutting off palms or heads, and
even heaping them up in triumph is referred to repeated-
ly. Also in art, heads and hands are depicted to symbolize
victory in battle." For more on this see *ANEP* illustrations
236 and 348. Also see Montet, *Everyday Life in Egypt*, 246,
in which he explains how the scribes would count these
trophies of war. First Samuel 18:27 shows how the He-
brews would cut off foreskins as trophies of war.

stand up for his own good actions to establish truth.[128]

(B1 325) Your rations are in your house;[129] your belly is full. The grain measurer[130] runs over; when it overflows the excess perishes on the ground. Those who seize one who is robbed are the plunderers. The officials who were appointed to repel evil should be shelters against aggressors, who are officials who were appointed to oppose falsehood.

No fear of you makes me appeal to you. You do not know my heart. (B1 330) The silent one, who returns to make a complaint to you, is not afraid to make his claim.[131] His likeness will not be brought to you from within the street. Your plots of land are in the country; your reward is in the estate; and your provisions are in the storehouse. The officials give to you, but you keep taking. Are you a thief, when one is brought in

---

128. This same phrase is used in (B1 233–234). The peasant is asking for help in establishing the truth of his appeal.

129. See Gardiner, 93, 7. This phrase was also used in [124–125]. The peasant rations are not in his house.

130. B1 325 has "grain measurer," but B2 57 has "barley."

131. The peasant is saying that he is not afraid.

before you, troops being together with you, for the divisions of the plots of land?

Do Truth for (B1 335) the Lord of Truth;
Truth exists in his Truth.
Pen, papyrus, and palette of Thoth,[132]
Avoid the doing of evil.
Beauty is beautiful when beauty is for him[133]
Now truth is for eternity;
It goes down with its doer to the necropolis.
When he is buried, (B1 340) the earth unites with him,
And his name is not smeared on earth.
He is remembered because of goodness;
This is the rule of the word of God.

132. Thoth was the god of writing but functioned in other capacities as well.

133. I think the "him" refers to the god, Thoth. The Egyptian reads, *nfr nfrt nfr r.f.* Here the poet is playing with words not only by sound but visually as well. The meaning of *nfr* can be, "good," "beautiful," "happy," or "well." Text B2 72 adds a fourth *nfr* and several translations read, "When goodness is good, goodness is good indeed." I translate "beauty" because of the relationship between "truth" and "beauty"; the focus of this poem is on truth.

This is a hand-balance; it does not tilt.[134] This is a stand-balance; it does not tilt to the side.[135] Look! If I (B1 345) come or if another comes, you[136] should answer. Do not answer with an answer of silence.[137] Do not attack one who cannot attack. You are not gentle; you are not troubled, yet, you do not destroy. But you did not give me a payment for (B1 350) this good speech, which comes from the mouth of Re himself.

> Speak Truth; do Truth.
> Since it is mighty; it is great;
> It endures; its trustworthiness is found;
> And it will pass on to a blessed state.

Does a hand-balance tilt? It is its pans that (B1 355) weigh things. There can be no excess to the rule.[138] A vile act cannot approach a town, nor can he who is at the back reach the land."

134. Here I follow the spelling in text B2 77.

135. See above in B1 179–180 for the hand-balance and the stand-balance. This present passage relates to the preceding mention of the "rule of the word of God," and the balance determines the truth of such a rule.

136. This refers to Rensi.

137. This is what Rensi is doing to the peasant.

138. The "rule" is mentioned above in B1 342.

The Ninth Appeal (from text B2)

(B2 91) And this peasant came to appeal to him a ninth time. He said, "Chief Steward, my Lord! The people's stand-balances[139] are their tongues. It is the hand-balance that searches out the deficiencies,[140] and inflicts punishment on the one to be punished. The rule is for you. (B2 95) Falsehood [goes astray] as is its due.[141] Truth brings it back and is equal to the items of falsehood. Truth causes renewed growth, though it has not been gathered.[142] When Falsehood departs, it goes astray; it does not cross over by ferry and has not [changed].[143] (B2 100) He who is made rich by it[144] has no children; he has

139. I try to keep the two kinds of balances consistent with the identification given in B1 179–180.

140. Or excess to the rule or standard as in B1 355. See note 138.

141. I have restored *tnm*, "goes astray." Parkinson (in *The Tale of the Eloquent Peasant*) says that the last letter looks like the owl (*m*), and this verb is used again in B2 97. But this is still just my best guess; the text is damaged at this point and in several more places here at the conclusion of the story.

142. B2 95–97 is left out by some, and all translations seem to be very tentative. Starting with B2 98 things become much clearer.

143. This word is uncertain.

144. "It" refers to Falsehood.

no heirs on earth. He who sails with it does not reach land; his boat does not moor at its town.

> Do not be heavy; you are not light.
>
> Do not be slow; you are not fast.
>
> Do not be partial; Do not listen to the heart.
>   (B2 105)
>
> Do not veil your face to one whom you know.
>
> Do not blind your face to one whom you have seen,
>
> Do not reject the poor man's claim against you, which you put down.
>
> Do not be idle; report your saying:
>
> *'Do for the one who does for you.'*[145]
>
> Do not listen to anyone who is against him;
>
> Summon such a man for his deeds to establish the Truth.[146]
>
> There is no yesterday for the negligent.[147] (B2 110)

145. See B1 141 in the second appeal for the peasant's golden rule, "Do for the doer to cause him to do." Here in B2 108, the recipient of such kindness is motivated to respond in like manner.

146. This line is like B1 234, ". . . helping a man stand up for his own good actions to establish Truth." The one, who responds to the golden rule, should be protected and summoned to establish his Truth. This is what the peasant has been doing.

147. He will not be remembered.

There is no friend for one who is deaf to the
    Truth.

There is no good day for the covetous.

The accuser becomes the wretched,

And the wretched becomes a pleader.

The opponent becomes a murderer.

Look, I am pleading with you, but you will
not hear it. I will go and plead (B2 115) concerning you to Anubis."[148]

Conclusion

Then the Chief Steward, Rensi, son of Meru, sent
two guards to bring him back. This peasant was
afraid. He thought it was decided to punish him
for this speech he had delivered.

This peasant said, "The approach of a thirsty
one for water, (B2 120) the stretching forth of
the mouth of an infant child for milk, this is
death. For him who prays to see it come, death is
delayed in coming for him."

---

148. Parkinson, 88 n. 110, explains, "*Anubis* is a god
of death and otherworldly judgement." Anubis is also pictured with Thoth as they participate in the weighing of
the heart at the judgment of the dead. See Steindorff and
Seele, *When Egypt Ruled the East*, 136 fig. 32. Here the
peasant threatens suicide. The peasant's name is Khun-
anup meaning "Anubis protects," and see n. 2 above.

The Chief Steward, Rensi, son of Meru said, "Peasant, do not fear! Look, you will prepare to deal with me."

This peasant gave cause,[149] (B2 125) "By my life, shall I eat from your bread[150] and drink your beer forever?"

The Chief Steward, Rensi, son of Meru said, "Now wait here and hear your petitions."

He had every petition read aloud from a new papyrus scroll in due course. (B2 130) The Chief Steward, Rensi, son of Meru delivered them to the majesty of the King of Upper and Lower Egypt, Nebkaure, true of voice.[151] They pleased his heart more than anything in the entire land.

His majesty said, "Render judgment yourself, son of Meru."

So, the Chief Steward, Rensi, son of Meru sent two guards to [get Nemtinakht].[152] (B2 135)

149. Most translators understand what follows as an oath, and they translate, "This peasant swore," but the verb here means "to give or cause." He gave vent to his frustration and asked a question in the form of a vow. This is not a serious oath.

150. Bread, as in Hebrew, could be translated as "food."

151. "True of voice" or "just of voice" means, "justified" or "deceased." It seems that this story is told after the death of Nebkaure.

152. It is clear that Rensi decided in favor of the peasant.

Then he was brought, and a list was made [. . .].[153]
Here he found six persons as well as [. . .] his Upper Egyptian barley, his emmer, his donkeys, his pigs, and his small cattle [. . .]. This Nemtinakht to this peasant [. . .][154] (B2 140) all his [. . .] of this Nemtinakht [. . .].

It is finished [from start to finish as found in writing].[155]

153. This was an inventory of Nemtinakht's property.

154. Apparently Nemtinakht has to give all of this property to the peasant.

155. The ending is in bad shape. I have not filled in the blanks as much as some do.

Conclusion

What a story! And written four thousand years ago! It is amazing that we can cross over a river of languages and centuries to enjoy and know something of life in ancient Egypt. Perhaps we need to ask if we have learned something about the peasant's life, or have we learned something about the storyteller's life? My answer is both. To be a good storyteller the protagonist must be pictured in realistic ways, and, at the same time, we must remember that the storyteller has a point of view and sometimes a hidden agenda.

Many people refer to this story as a Wisdom Tale, and it does teach the importance of good speech and truth. The idea of perfect speech was a constant theme in Egypt's didactic literature. In *The Instruction for King Merikare*, from about the same period as our story, we have:

> If you are skilled in speech, you will win.
> The tongue is [a king's] sword;

Speaking is stronger than all fighting.

The skillful is not overcome.[1]

In Genesis, Joseph is portrayed as a perfect administrator for Egypt, and the storyteller in Genesis knows just how to paint his portrait. He must have perfect speech. In Genesis 37:4 we note that Joseph's brothers are jealous of him:

> His brothers saw that their father loved him more than any of his brothers. They hated him, and they could not overcome his perfect speech.[2]

My translation of this passage is easy, but most ancient and recent translators have made the mistake of assuming that the "speech" in this verse is that of the brothers. To do this they have to change the Hebrew text. Joseph's speech was perfect, and for this portrait he was dressed in fine Egyptian linen.

As to the genre of our story I call it prose. Parkinson sees it as poetry.[3] My understanding is informed by Lichtheim's analysis. She claims that Egyptian literature employs three styles: prose, orational style, and poetry. Then she says,

1. Lichtheim, 1:99. Also see Wilson, 415; *COS* 1.35, 62; and Fisher, *Genesis, A Royal Epic*, 168 n. 4.

2. Fisher, ibid., 168.

3. Parkinson, 54–88.

"If prose is to poetry as walking is to dancing, the intermediate style may be compared to the formal parade step."[4] *The Eloquent Peasant* is a prose tale, which contains poetry and the intermediate style.

Finally, I would like to emphasize again that for me this story is another "Flash of Freedom" and a contribution to the growth of civilization.[5] However such growth has its ups and downs. This story was popular in the Middle Kingdom, but the growth of the Empire did not help:

> Did social justice help the pharaoh's plan?
> A loyal follower was his demand.
> The New Empire's love was for expansion,
> And human rights were not in its mission.

> The adventurous gave us these insights.
> They looked beyond safe limits and their plight.
> Their learning was essential for nurture,
> But imagination brought adventure.

> Their flashes of freedom are to be treasured.
> Lightning is fertile, not to be measured.

4. Lichtheim, 1:11.

5. Fisher, *Tales from Ancient Egypt*, 90–92.

Ours to remember: "In any kingdom,
Altar, Greed, and Empire kill flashes of
freedom."[6]

6. Ibid.

Epilogue

The Eloquent Peasant and the
Creation of Humans

This title calls to mind Harold Bloom's book, *Shakespeare, the Invention of the Human*.[1] Bloom says that Shakespeare went beyond all others (even Chaucer) and "invented the human as we continue to know it." After translating *The Eloquent Peasant*, however, I have concluded that Harold Bloom's interest in Shakespeare's universalism is commendable, but this universalism has a long and interesting history.

It is easy to understand how the peasant could paint such an accurate portrait of the bureaucrats of his day. They were against him at every turn on his way to justice. Before the peasant made his first appeal, Rensi accused Nemtinakht of robbing and beating the peasant, but the officials discounted

---

1. Bloom, *Shakespeare, the Invention of the Human* (New York: Riverhead, 1998) xviii.

the seriousness of the accusation. Nevertheless, Rensi wanted to hear the peasant's appeals.

The metaphorical story of good sailing on the Lake of Truth in the first appeal (p. 13) sets the tone and the goal of the subsequent speeches—minus the sharp criticism that increased after a beating by the court guards (p. 29). Good sailing for the creator of truth includes caring for the widow and the orphan and hearing the cry of the afflicted, "I speak that you may hear; create truth, . . . Examine me" (p. 14).

In the second appeal, the peasant notes, "justice flees" from the bureaucrats, who practice "crafty speech" and steal, and you, Rensi, are not helping. "Do for the doer to cause him to do" (p. 20). "Save the shipwrecked; save me."

The third appeal is central to the peasant's thought. "Doing justice! This is breath in the nose" (p. 25). This creates human beings. Four thousand years ago a peasant is credited with this great truth: The human is not "invented" but rather created by doing and receiving justice. And how does the ruler dispense justice? The peasant's answer: by being a good sailor and a true balance that weighs actions against truth and justice. Control the flood in order to do justice; "making equal the land is doing justice (p 26)."

In subsequent appeals it becomes clear that one's humanity not only involves doing justice to one's fellows, but it also assumes that you treat the land with kindness. There is this built-in equation: your care with truth and justice for the environment equals your care for all living beings. There is too much hunting and fishing (pp. 31 and 33).

Environmental regulations protect the poor and the powerless. The god Thoth is not partial, and you must not be partial. "Do truth for the Lord of Truth" (p. 41). Know that truth is for eternity. So, human beings should speak out. "The peoples stand-balances are their tongues" (p. 43). After the peasant's first speech, Rensi said to the king, "I have found one from these peasants whose beautiful speech is a reality." Notice there must be no gap between the speech and the reality, and thus it is beautiful. A. N. Whitehead would welcome this understanding for he said, "[Truth] is the conformation of Appearance to Reality."[2]

Charles Hartshorne, in his *Omnipotence and Other Theological Mistakes*,[3] tells us that

2. Whitehead, *Adventures of Ideas* (New York: The Free Press, 1967) 265.

3. Hartshorne, *Omnipotence and Other Theological Mistakes* (Albany: State University of New York, 1984) 109.

Whitehead, other process thinkers, and contemporary physicists conclude that reality consists of "events not things." Hebrew views concerning creation were not overly interested in things or matter but in their God creating order out of chaos. For them, this was a creative event. The realities, in the life of the Hebrew state or in lives of individuals, were a series of events or actual occasions of experience.[4] If someone builds a brick wall, the bricks are necessary, but the reality is complex; it involves motivation, planning, and building. The reality depends on a series of events.

Above I quoted, "Do for the doer to cause him to do." This ancient form of the Golden Rule is not a descriptive form. It is full of verbal action; it is an event, and it will become a reality. In the third appeal, we see the importance of doing justice. "This is breath to the nose." In the Hebrew Bible, we know the meaning of this expression. In Genesis 2:7, God blew into the nostrils of the human the breath of life, and the human became a living being. Somehow breath to the nose makes one truly human. Doing and

---

4. These experiences and actions are narrated with verbs (sometimes in the causative), and they are not just described in nominal sentences. This is also the case for other Semitic languages in the east Mediterranean.

receiving justice is that which makes one truly human. It is another event, and it has to do with reality.

In subsequent appeals it becomes clear that one's humanity not only involves doing justice to one's fellows, but it also assumes that you treat the land with kindness. Your care with truth and justice for the environment equals your care for all living beings. Environmental regulations protect the poor and the powerless.

The peasant's perfect speech was true and beautiful, because each word conformed to the realities of events as he experienced them. The peasant knew that truth and justice created human beings, free speech, environmental or "land ethics," and beauty. We must credit these humans from 2000 BCE for their insights and their adventurous attempts to better their world. For us, this story is about the creation and evolution of human beings and their home.

Bibliography

Buck, A. de. *Egyptian Reading Book: Exercises and Middle Egyptian Texts*. Vol. 1. Leiden: Nederlandsch Archaeologisch Instituut Voor Het Nabije Oosten, 1948.

Drioton, Étienne, and Jacques Vandier. *L'Égypte*. "CLIO," Les Peuples de l'Orient Méditerranéen II. Paris: Presses Universitaires de France, 1952.

Erman, Adolf, and Hermann Grapow. *Wörterbuch der ägyptischen Sprache: Zur Geschichte eines grossen wissenschaftlichen Unternehmens der Akademie*. Deutsche Akademie der Wissenschaften zu Berlin: Vorträge und Schriften 51. Berlin: Akademie, 1955.

Faulkner, R. O. "The Tale of the Eloquent Peasant." In *The Literature of Ancient Egypt*, edited by William Kelly Simpson, 31–49. New ed. New Haven: Yale University Press, 1973.

Fisher, Loren R. *Genesis, A Royal Epic*. 2nd ed. Eugene, OR: Cascade Books, 2011.

———. *The Jerusalem Academy*. 2nd ed. Eugene, OR: Wipf & Stock, 2012.

———. *Living without Justice*. Eugene, OR: Wipf & Stock, 2013.

———. *The Many Voices of Job*. Eugene, OR: Cascade Books, 2009.

———. *The Minority Report: Silenced by Religion*. 2nd ed. Eugene, OR: Wipf & Stock, 2013.

———. *The Rebel Job*. Rev. ed. Walnut Creek, CA: BookSurge, 2009.

———. *Tales from Ancient Egypt: The Birth of Stories*. Eugene, OR: Cascade Books, 2010.

Gardiner, Alan H., Sir. *Egypt of the Pharaohs*. Oxford: Clarendon, 1961.

———. *Egyptian Grammar*. 2nd ed. London: Oxford University Press, 1950.

———. *Late-Egyptian Stories*. Bibliotheca Aegyptiaca 1. Brussels: Édition de la Fondation Égyptologique Reine Élisabeth, 1932. Reprinted, 1973.

Gordon, Cyrus H. *Adventures in the Nearest East*. London: Phoenix House, 1957.

———. *Before The Bible*. New York: Harper & Row, 1962.

———. *The Common Background of Greek and Hebrew Civilizations*. New York: Norton, 1965.

———. *Ugaritic Textbook*. Analecta Orientalia 38. Rome: Pontifical Biblical Institute, 1965.

———. *The World of the Old Testament*. Garden City: Doubleday, 1958.

Gordon, Cyrus H., and Gary A. Rendsburg. *The Bible and the Ancient Near East*. 4th ed. New York: Norton, 1997.

Hallo, William W. et al., editors. *The Context of Scripture*. Vols. 1 and 2. Leiden: Brill, 1997, 2000.

Homan, Michael M. "Beer and Its Drinkers: An Ancient Near Eastern Love Story." *NEA* 67 (2004) 84–95.

Lichtheim, Miriam. *Ancient Egyptian Literature*. Vol. 1. Berkeley: The University of California Press, 1975.

———. *Ancient Egyptian Literature*. Vol. 2. Berkeley: University of California Press, 1976.

Montet, Pierre. *Everyday Life in Egypt in the Days of Ramesses the Great*. Translated by A. R. Maxwell-Hyslop and Margaret S. Drower. New York: St. Martin's, 1958.

Moran, William L. *The Amarna Letters*. Baltimore: Johns Hopkins University Press, 1992.

Parkinson, R. B. *The Tale of the Eloquent Peasant*. Oxford: Griffith Institute / Ashmolean Museum, 1991.

———. *The Tale of Sinuhe and Other Egyptian Poems 1940–1640 BC*. Oxford World's Classics. Oxford: Oxford University Press, 1997 (paperback ed., 2009).

Pritchard, James B., ed. *The Ancient Near East in Pictures Relating to the Old Testament*. Princeton: Princeton University Press, 1954. 2nd ed., 1969.

———, ed. *Ancient Near Eastern Texts Relating to the Old Testament*. 3rd ed. Princeton: Princeton University Press, 1969.

Pope, Marvin H. *Job*. 3rd. ed. Anchor Bible 15. Garden City, NY: Doubleday, 1973.

Bibliography

Rainey, A. F. "The World of Sinuhe." *Israel Oriental Studies* 2 (1972) 369–408.

Rendsburg, Gary A. "Inaugural Lecture: The Genesis of the Bible." New Brunswick: Rutgers, The State University of New Jersey, 2004.

Simpson, William Kelly. "The Shipwrecked Sailor" and "The Story of Sinuhe." *The Literature of Ancient Egypt: An Anthology of Stories, Instructions, and Poetry*, edited by William Kelly Simpson, 50–56. New ed. New Haven: Yale University Press, 1973.

———. "The Story of Sinuhe." In *The Literature of Ancient Egypt*, edited by William Kelly Simpson, 57–74. New ed. New Haven: Yale University Press, 1973.

Steindorff, George, and Keith C. Seele. *When Egypt Ruled the East*. 2nd ed. Chicago: University of Chicago Press, 1957.

Ward, W. A. ""The Egyptian Office of Joseph." *Journal of Semitic Studies* 5 (1960) 144–50.

Wente, Edward F. Jr. "A Note on *The Eloquent Peasant*, B 1, 13–15." *Journal of Near Eastern Studies* 24 (1965) 105–9.

———. "The Report of Wenamon." In *The Literature of Ancient Egypt*, edited by William Kelly Simpson, 142–55. New ed. New Haven: Yale University Press, 1973.

———. "The Tale of the Doomed Prince" and "The Report of Wenamon." In *The Literature of Ancient Egypt*, edited by William Kelly Simpson, 65–91. New ed. New Haven: Yale University Press, 1973.

Whitehead, Alfred North. *Adventures of Ideas*. New York: Free Press, 1967.

Wilson, John A. *The Burden of Egypt*. Chicago: University of Chicago Press, 1951.

———. *The Culture of Ancient Egypt*. Chicago: University of Chicago Press, 1956.

———. "A Dispute Over Suicide." In *Ancient Near Eastern Texts Relating to the Old Testament*, edited by James B. Pritchard, 405–7. 3rd ed. Princeton: Princeton University Press, 1969.

———. "The Journey of Wen-Amon to Phoenicia." In *Ancient Near Eastern Texts Relating to the Old Testament*, edited by James B. Pritchard, 25–29. 3rd ed. Princeton: Princeton University Press, 1969.

———. "The Protests of The Eloquent Peasant." In *Ancient Near Eastern Texts Relating to the Old Testament*, edited by

James B. Pritchard, 407–10. 3rd ed. Princeton: Princeton University Press, 1969.

———. "The Repulsing of the Dragon." In *Ancient Near Eastern Texts Relating to the Old Testament*, edited by James B. Pritchard, 11–12. 3rd ed. Princeton: Princeton University Press, 1969.

———. "The Story of Si-nuhe." In *Ancient Near Eastern Texts Relating to the Old Testament*, edited by James B. Pritchard, 18–22. 3rd ed. Princeton: Princeton University Press, 1969.

Index of Ancient Documents

❧

Index of Ancient Documents

Made in the USA
Monee, IL
04 February 2021